Around
Woodbridge

IN OLD PHOTOGRAPHS

An old print of Woodbridge as seen from the Sutton shore of the Deben river. Two windmills can be seen top right and another top left, by the church. In Edward Fitzgerald's time there were three windmills on the hill, and when one of them was in danger of demolition he bought the land in order to save it. During the sixteenth and seventeenth centuries Woodbridge experienced fire damage, piracy, plagues and witch hunts.

Around Woodbridge

IN OLD PHOTOGRAPHS

Collected by
HUMPHREY PHELPS

Alan Sutton Publishing Limited
Phoenix Mill · Far Thrupp · Stroud
Gloucestershire

First Published 1992

**British Library Cataloguing
in Publication Data**

Phelps, Humphrey
  Around Woodbridge in Old Photographs
  I. Title
  942.646

ISBN 0–7509–0110–1

Typeset in 9/10 Sabon.
Typesetting and origination by
Alan Sutton Publishing Limited.
Printed in Great Britain by
The Bath Press, Avon.

Contents

Introduction

For most of the period covered by this book, the sea and farming dominated the lives of many of the people of the district; if not the sea or farming, then the rivers and associated trades. Woodbridge itself was once a busy port and a market town; today it may have lost most of the vitality that sprang naturally from its environment but it remains a place of enchantment, neither too big nor too small. To wander round the town, to see the Thoroughfare on a late afternoon in winter with the lights twinkling, is to experience delight. And who can fail to find enchantment in the other places in this book? Orford, for instance, which always seems to be smiling. I speak as one who fell in love with this whole district many years ago, and despite the changes that have occurred during the intervening years I have an irresistible urge to revisit the area at every available opportunity.

There have been losses and it is all too easy to become nostalgic while looking at these photographs, but we should remember there have been gains as well. Whether the gains outnumber the losses or vice versa is debatable. Perhaps Charles Dickens got it right about this or any other period when he wrote, 'It was the best of times, it was the worst of times.'

The photographs have been divided into sections. The first four sections are topographical, to set the scene as it were, but by far the largest section is of people and occasions, people being in my opinion the most interesting subject. As Alexander Pope said, 'The proper study of mankind is man.' A small section follows on education. There are a number of photographs of one particular school and for good reasons. This school's photographs are a fine example of what a good, rural education for country children could be. All too often, and especially today, village schooling has tended to make country children think the centre of existence is town.

However, we cannot ignore the fact that today there is very little employment in country districts; consequently country children have small chance of developing into country men or women. Part of the reason for this is to be found in the agricultural section. The photographs illustrate how people accomplished what they did in years gone by. Work was done by many hands, by the muscle of men and horses. Slow and laborious, but not so slow and laborious as we may suppose. The work was done steadily but surely with none of the delays occasioned by the breakdown of sophisticated and expensive machinery. Laborious, yes, but not so laborious as it must appear to an untutored observer. Companionship, rhythm and skill helped to lighten the toil, although it must be admitted that the living conditions and wages were often appallingly poor. The farms themselves gave employment to other country people – wheelwrights, blacksmiths, harness makers, millers and other tradesmen – so work and money stayed in the district instead of disappearing into large towns.

The last section illustrates some of the mills in the district. They remind us of a time when almost every Suffolk parish had one or more windmills, their sails turning in the wind. Free power and power free from pollution, beauty and use in one. While looking at these pictures I have been impressed by the way in which beauty and utility were combined.

And how well dressed most of the people were, although many must have suffered hardship and privation. Equally impressive is the strong bond of community which must have existed, and the capacity of people to make their own amusements and pleasures, usually springing directly from their work: harvest frolics and outings, horse shows, and so forth.

I have included little of the immediate effects of wars or other disasters. By some this may be counted as a fault, but like George Bourne I hold that 'How people live, and not how they are disturbed in living, is the important thing.'

While I expect many readers will regret with me some of the changes and some of the losses, we should console ourselves that this district has been fortunate in many ways. It still has its coastline and sea, even if the latter is still devouring the former as it has done for centuries past. It still has those high skies and that luminous clarity so beloved of artists (and that includes photographers). It still has woodlands and wetlands, heath and rivers, and that quality so difficult to define which makes it such a delightful district. For this we should be thankful, but thankfulness is not enough; constant vigilance is needed to keep it the way it is. And please remember that today's snapshots will be tomorrow's old photographs.

Of the many pleasures I have enjoyed while compiling this collection, a major one has been meeting the descendants of those who have really created this book. May readers enjoy some of the pleasure I have experienced. I should like to thank all those who have invited me into their homes and trusted me by lending me their treasured photographs. To all these, to all those who have helped in so many ways, I tender my grateful and sincere thanks.

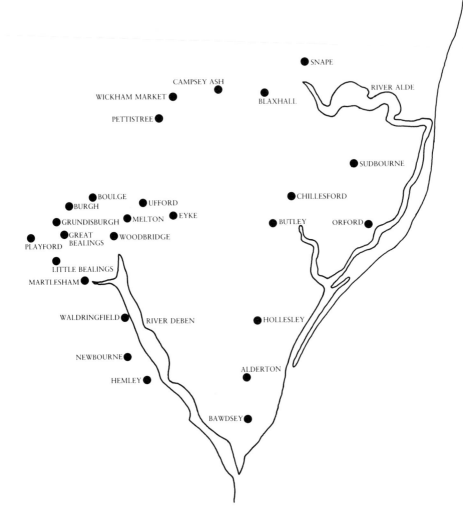

Map showing places covered in the book.

SECTION ONE

Woodbridge

This Woodbridge, with its capital Air.
Edward Fitzgerald

Woodbridge and the Deben seen from a similar vantage point as the print on p. 2 but at a much later date. 'My chief amusement in Life is Boating, on River and Sea,' said Edward Fitzgerald. He went to live in Woodbridge in 1860 and spent much of his time in his small yacht which he named *The Scandal*. Scandal, he alleged, was Woodbridge's main commodity.

Edward Fitzgerald. Best known for his translation into English verse of *The Rubaiyat of Omar Khayyam*, Fitzgerald was born at Bredfield in 1809. Distressed by the condition of farm workers during the 1840s, he started giving some of their wives small allowances. He spent fourteen years in lodgings in the centre of Woodbridge and found them 'cheerful, warm and convenient (only the Privy quite public)'. Fitzgerald was 6ft tall and had bright blue eyes, rugged features and bushy eyebrows. Indoors he would sit in a dressing gown and wear a top hat. Out of doors he wore a baggy blue suit, a plaid shawl and a hat tied to his head with a handkerchief.

The Bell and Steelyard Inn, New Street, a Tudor building with an eighteenth-century casement. Its most prominent feature, the steelyard, was a seventeenth-century addition. It was used for weighing loads of produce such as corn, hay, hides or wool (the town was an important wool centre). The loaded wagon was hoisted and suspended by pulley and chain and then counterpoised by moving a weight along the notched beam to tell the weight of the load. In 1897 the steelyard was taken to London for the Victorian Era Exhibition and then returned to its present position. At various times the inn has been called The Three Goats, Stillyards, Fox, Bell, and Bluebell. Milk is being delivered on the left by horse and float. The milk was taken out of the churns with a measure and poured into the householder's jug. If the milk in the churns was not kept well agitated later customers' milk would contain little of the cream.

A later photograph of the Bell and Steelyard Inn with a much better view of the steelyard. The country's only other surviving steelyard is at Soham, Isle of Ely.

In The Thoroughfare (or Thoro'fare), 1869. A bookseller is offering an apple by way of encouragement to a hard-pressed horse. To the crowd he said, 'When you have a difficulty with man or beast, don't use the whip but show him the apple.'

The Thoroughfare, early 1900s. The Cross Inn is on the left, the Crown on the right. The Street, devoid of vehicles, allows the people to go about their business in a peaceful manner or even, perhaps, to indulge in what Fitzgerald alleged was the town's 'main commodity'. A Royal Navy sailor is on the right, a boy with a tray of plants on the left. Women are in long dresses, boys in knickerbockers and stockings. This principal street is almost a mile in length.

The Thoroughfare, 1900, with Horace Reynolds directing the traffic. The Crown Hotel is on the left.

Funeral procession, The Thoroughfare, 1910. The coffin of Horace Reynolds is being carried over the place where he used to direct traffic. He was thirty-two years of age when he died.

J. Betts and Son's pharmacy in The Thoroughfare, *c.* 1908. There is still a pharmacy at these premises today. Note the sign for 'Petrol' on the right.

The Thoroughfare, late 1940s. In 1929 the *Suffolk Chronicle* said 'the traffic problem is one of some consequence.' In this picture it consists of just one small Ford van, probably because petrol was still severely rationed. At this time scarves had become fashionable head-dresses for women.

TYSON & SON

Grocers.   Provision Merchants.

FREE OF RATION.

COOKED BACON

2/4 per lb.

THORO'FARE, WOODBRIDGE

Advertisement in *Woodbridge Reporter* and *Wickham Market Gazette*, 5 October 1944. Food was rationed, so why was this bacon free of ration?

Market Hill and the Shire Hall, *c.* 1920s. The Shire Hall was built in 1575 by Thomas Seckford (the Seckford Arms are above the doorway) and the County Sessions were moved here from Melton. Originally the ground floor was not enclosed and was used as a market. Trading was also done in the churchyard, but in 1585 Humphrey Seckford must have gone too far as he was fined for selling cattle and pigs there. The Shire Hall was also used as a gaol and the twin iron gates of the cells can be seen either side of the great doorway. Until recently, an upper part of the hall, with access on the other and higher side, was used as a magistrates' court. After the break up of his marriage, Edward Fitzgerald went to live in a house on Market Hill (now marked with a plaque). When his friend, Alfred Tennyson, visited him, he put up at The Bull, just below the Shire Hall. John Grout, the landlord, was an authority on horses and showed Tennyson round his stables. On being informed later by Fitzgerald that he had had the Poet Laureate at his inn, he retorted, 'He didn't fare to know anything about horses.'

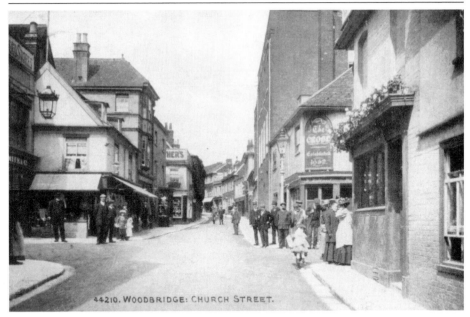

Church Street, formerly known as Stone Street.

Built during the seventeenth century, the Bull Inn always had a close association with horses. George Carlow, an ostler, was buried near its stables rather than in the church-yard.

The ferry. The postman is crossing the River Deben near the Tide Mill to deliver mail in the Sutton district.

The King's Arms, 1950s. The name of this public house will serve as an excuse to relate the strange story of the head of the man involved in a king losing his head. On the death of Oliver Cromwell, his body was embalmed and buried in Westminster Abbey, but at the Restoration it was disinterred and the head was kept at Westminster Hall for years. It then passed through many hands until eventually it came into the possession of the Wilkinson family at Woodbridge. Thorough investigations showed that it was undoubtedly Cromwell's head. It was finally buried in the church of Sydney Sussex, Cambridge, Cromwell's old college.

Ferry Quay and tide mill. A tide mill has stood on this site since 1170. The mill seen here was built in 1793 and continued working until 1957. It was the last working tide mill in the country. It fell into disrepair but has now been restored and is open to the public from May to September every day except Monday. The roof of the building second from the left bears the name 'Whisstock'. Whisstock's Boatyard was the best known in East Suffolk. In 1937 it started its own class boat, and during the Second World War built over two hundred craft for the war effort.

First shelter and tide mill.

WOODBRIDGE.—THE QUAY

The Quay, *c.* 1900. A Custom House was built on the Quay in 1589, but by the latter part of the seventeenth century the Custom House was in Quay Street. At that period the annual revenue on Suffolk cloth alone amounted to almost £3,000. The tide mill is far right.

Bandstand and River Wall, Woodbridge

Weldon's Series

The bandstand and river wall, *c.* 1900.

The beach in the early twentieth century.

Wilford Bridge. 'Oh for to sit upon the banks of the dear old Deben, with the worthy collier's sloop going forth into the wide world.' (Edward Fitzgerald). There were three hundred mariners and thirteen ships from Woodbridge at the Siege of Calais; three of its ships joined the English Fleet to intercept the Armada. In 1940, as soon as the appeal was made, two yachts from Woodbridge went to assist in the Dunkirk evacuation.

The Promenade, *c.* 1935.

The jetty, *c.* 1930.

Woodbridge Railway Station and the River Deben, *c.* 1910, with horse carriages awaiting trains on the left. In the mid-nineteenth century Woodbridge had twenty-three boat makers, two coach makers, five corn millers, seven maltsters, thirty-five master mariners, two sail makers, two wheelwrights, three stay makers, seven straw-hat makers, twenty-four inns and nine beerhouses.

Little Grange. In 1873 Edward Fitzgerald left Market Hill and went to Little Grange (Pythes Road), the last of his homes. He died in 1883 and is buried in Bougle churchyard.

St John's Hill, August 1916. There was a Zeppelin raid on Woodbridge on 12 August 1916. The first bombs fell at St John's Hill. Six people were killed. Several properties were shattered and the blast tore away the face of the church clock.

Ruins caused by the same raid. A total of twenty-eight bombs fell on Woodbridge in the night. The doorway marked 'X' is where Mr and Mrs Tyler were killed. Apparently, when the church bells rang a warning of the raid Mr and Mrs Tyler came to the doorway to see the Zeppelin – their three children upstairs survived.

Seckford Almshouses, named after Thomas Seckford, a wealthy sixteenth-century merchant and Woodbridge benefactor, who had a brilliant legal career. His charity paid – and still pays – for almshouses, hospital, dispensary, grammar school, library. His brother, Henry, was a pirate, and Thomas himself was accused of being engaged in piracy, fraud and smuggling.

THE PHYLLIS MEMORIAL HOME MELTON
WOODBRIDGE

BIRTH
ANNOUNCEMENT

The Phyllis Memorial Home, opened in 1929. It was given to the district by Sir William and Lady Churchman in memory of their daughter Phyllis, who died in childbirth. Despite being much loved by the district and ten thousand people signing a petition to save it, it is now closed.

Bandstand and shelters, *c.* 1900.

Melton Grange.

Melton Street, *c.* 1910. The shopkeeper waits upon the man and woman in the trap while a boy holds the head of the horse in the trap behind. The iron railings were probably made at the Wickham Market Ironworks.

The Horse and Groom, Melton. 'Cobbold's beer, motors on hire, cycles to let.' And a double-deck motor omnibus to take local people to Ipswich. Some passengers seem more intent on being in the photograph than on the omnibus. And we must not forget the little girl with a baby in the pram. In 1844 an omnibus ran from the Coach and Horses to meet the London steamers at Ipswich.

The Coach and Horses and Melton Brewery, *c.* 1890. Cuthbert Quilter of Bawdsey Manor, MP for South Suffolk in 1885, was an advocate of pure food and beer, the beer to be made solely of barley, malt and hops – and presumably of pure water. His Bill to ensure all beer was made in this way did not succeed so for a time he had this brewery at Melton. In 1844 there were three maltsters at Melton, one brewer who was also a baker, three inns, one beerhouse, one miller, a harness maker, a millwright and a blacksmith who was also a wheelwright.

The tide mill, *c.* 1950.

SECTION TWO

Wickham Market

Thence to Wickham five mile more – but these are all very long miles.
Celia Fiennes

Permit me, dear sister, to greet you once more
Not from shady retreats but from Aldeburgh's rough shore,
Through Woodbridge and Wickham our post horses rattled
Whilst the ride we enjoyed and incessantly prattled.
'Twas a custom in Suffolk, I've heard travellers tell,
To drink health to all friends who lived round Wickham well;
I am sure sister Sarah was ready to jump
When she found the old well was transformed to a pump.

(*A lady's tour from Canonbury to Aldeburgh*, from *Old Suffolk Garland*)

Wickham Market church, *c.* 1902. The tower is of a type rare in Suffolk. 'The Church and spire-steeple are situated upon a hill; and, though the steeple is not above twenty-three yards high, in a clear day you may easily view from hence very near, if not altogether, fifty churches.' (John Kirby, *Suffolk Traveller*). It is generally agreed that John Kirby must have had extraordinarily powerful eyesight.

Market Hill, *c.* 1916. Posing for the camera.

The Hill, focal point of Wickham. The pump by the pole on the left supplied pure ice-cold drinking water all year for all the surrounding households and was the sole supply until 1939 or even later. Note the water cart. Behind the nearest pole is Revell's butchers shop. The Blew Boare stood here, it was where the Cavalier parson of Letheringham drank deeply of spiritous liquor in 1644 and scandalized the Puritan parishioners of Charsfield. They said he often fell into the hedges on his way home. Little Dick, the Campsea Ash smuggler, was also an habitué of the Blew Boare. Doubtless, the local inhabitants had lots of gossip over the years as they gathered to wait their turn at the pump.

Glenering Bridge, on the road to Easton.

The market developed here and went as far up as the White Hart. Mr Taylor's dairy was here in the 1930s; he was also a shoemaker, a harness maker, and a clock maker. Far right is Adam's bakery. People are about to board a bus, and there are prams, handcarts and bicycles.

W. Taylor's shop, 1916. Mrs Taylor, attired for the foulest weather and assisted by a very able-looking young man, is about to deliver milk in the milk pram. Mr Taylor was serving in the Navy at this period. Note the 17 gallon wide-based churn in the pram and the smaller container which the young man carries.

The White Hart, 1950s, a fifteenth-century coaching house with eighteenth-century eleva-
tions. One bedroom was once a hayloft. In 1810 the innkeeper, Thomas Keepener,
wagered a visiting nobleman that he could drive a coach-and-four from Wickham to
Norwich and back (a round journey of about eighty miles) in five hours. On the day he set
off the Market Square was crowded with sightseers from all around the district at 8 a.m.
Thomas Keepener won his wager with a quarter of an hour to spare. In 1831 a number of
local farmers met at the White Hart and founded the East Suffolk Agricultural Society and
planned the first Suffolk Agricultural Show which was staged at Wickham on 21
September 1832 at the farm of Cornelis Walton, the Secretary. After that the show was
held alternately at Wickham and Saxmundham until 1845. At the Wickham show in
1838, 'three hundred and ninety gentlemen partook of an elegant entertainment provided
by Mr Tye of the White Hart'. It was then that the Earl of Stradbroke said that he 'was
looking forward to the time when they should plough without horses'. A prize of £2 was
given 'to the labourer in Husbandry . . . by whom the greatest number of legitimate children has been brought up, with or without the least parochial relief'. In 1832 'the biggest
family' winner was Robert Taylor of Hollesley with eleven legitimate children and no
parish relief. When the show was held at Framlingham in 1860 the winner had eighteen
children. By 1900, when the show was at Woodbridge, 'big family' prizes had ceased. In
that year's catalogue one advertisement read, 'H. Edwards of the Thorofare has fine
Scotch. 5 per cent under proof 21s. per gallon, 3s. 6d. a bottle.'

The Hill, 1920. A wheel seems to be coming off the small cart in the centre. To its left are some tar barrels, and beside them is the apparatus for heating tar and a cart wheel.

Another view of The Hill in the 1920s. The communal pump is just in front of the motor bus, a group of people and a pram are in the centre, and a rather 'dashing' motor car on the left.

Snowden Hill, late 1920s. The cartridges and tea signs are outside H.G. Parker's chemists shop. The two women on the right are standing by Lynn House where Dr Lehanann lived. Next is the post office (later used by Lloyds Bank). Cook's Bakery is almost obscured. Miss Finch had her dressmaking business in this street, and Snowden House, the home of John Whitmore, the Wickham industrialist, was here.

Bordercot Corner, The Street. The Victoria Jubilee Pump was erected here in 1897 to provide drinking water for the inhabitants of Lower Wickham. Unfortunately, the water was so heavily impregnated with iron it was unfit to drink. The motor car is outside Castell's Garage.

The Street and post office (now Barclays Bank), early 1900s. The George Inn, left, and the ivy-covered house at the foot of Snowden Hill were destroyed by bombs.

High Street, 1930s. Neslings Garage is on the left.

Norfolk Terrace. A German raider bombed this street in October 1942. Three people were killed and several houses (marked 'X' on photograph) were destroyed.

Middle Street was also bombed and the houses which were destroyed are marked 'X'.

Bridge Street in the 1920s. Whitmore & Binyon's Engineering Works was situated in this street. The Ironworks founded by Whitmore in 1780 flourished, and was at its height from 1818 onwards. The firm specialized in mill machinery. 'Wickham Market is celebrated for building windmills and for its manufacture of mill machinery. Mr Whitmore, the manufacturer, has exported within the last three years three fine windmills to the Continent, and one to South Australia, one to Van Dieman's Land, and one to New Zealand.' (The Post Office Directory, 1846). The Ironworks made other iron products, including iron gates and railings. It closed in 1903.

The bridge by the watermill, 1920s.

Bridge Street, 1930s. Waterloo Terrace is covered with ivy. Waterloo House was built in the 1820s. Beyond is Holden House and beyond that is the site of the Ironworks office. Next is the Gospel Hall. The Volunteer public house sign can just be seen on the left; it was named after the local volunteer force raised in 1859.

Roadworks in Dallinghoo Road, *c.* 1920. Wickham church spire is in the background. In 1843 Wickham had a cooper, a whitesmith, a basket maker, a gun maker, a coachbuilder, a brick and tile maker, a harness maker, a straw-hat maker, a clock maker, three black-smiths, seven bootmakers, and the Ironworks. Ninety years on there were a blacksmith, a bootmaker, a wattle maker, a thatcher, a miller, a saddler, a carriage builder, a wheel-wright and a clock maker.

SECTION THREE

Grundisburgh to
Waldringfield

The Suffolk skies are pale and bright,
Its ocean airs are keen.
                    Sir Francis Newbolt

Grundisburgh, c. 1912. 'It occurs to me that, when I last saw you, you gave me hopes of finding a Chanticleer to replace the aged fellow you saw in my Domains. He came from Grundisburgh and surely you spoke of some such Bird flourishing in Grundisburgh still. I will not hold out for the identical plumage – worthy of an Archangel . . .' (Edward Fitzgerald in a letter of December 1877 to Hermann Biddell). Biddell used to visit Fitzgerald on Woodbridge market days.

Houses at Grundisburgh, c. 1900. In the centre a man is carrying an unidentified load on his shoulders.

The Half Moon Inn, Grundisburgh, 1929.

The Dog Inn, Grundisburgh, 1920s. Both these inns are listed in White's 1844 *Suffolk Directory*. John Pyke kept The Dog and Charles Stearn kept the Half Moon. The village also had two beerhouses.

The Green, Grundisburgh

The Green, Grundisburgh, *c.* 1900s. Showing the old post office, and the old school far right. The school was built in 1872 and was one of the first Board Schools in Suffolk. A new school was opened a few years ago and the old one is now a listed building. This village enjoyed what one might call an idyllic arrangement; around the Green at different periods were: church, school, post office, Dog Inn, smithy and reading room, the pond and houses. At the time of the photograph the principal employers were farms, the two smithys, the windmill, and the basket makers, coopers and shoemakers. Grundisburgh Hall was the seat of the Blois family until they moved to Yoxford, and since 1844 it has been the home of the Gurdons, who became the Lord Cranworths. The forge, which was once responsible for the shoeing of a hundred horses, has been moved and re-erected at the Museum of Rural Life at Stowmarket. In 1844 the village had a corn miller, two blacksmiths, two wheelwrights and a basket maker. Ninety years later there was a blacksmith, a saddler, a basket maker and two wheelwrights. (These figures, like others given for the same periods elsewhere, only refer to businesses, not employees.)

The Street, Grundisburgh, looking towards the Green, *c.* 1900. The four Biddell brothers went to a small school in Grundisburgh. Manfred (the eldest) became a successful farmer and horse breeder and the first treasurer to the Suffolk Stud Book Association. George was noted for his agricultural inventions and as a civil engineer. William became MP for West Suffolk in the 1870s and was known as the 'Tenant Farmers' MP'. Herman compiled Volume One of the *Suffolk Horse Stud Book*: *a History and Register of the County Breed of Cart Horses* (1880).

The Rectory, Grundisburgh *c.* 1914.

The pond, Grundisburgh, *c*. 1900, showing Weir Farm.

The Half Moon Inn, Grundisburgh, *c*. 1900. Traps could be hired from the inn in the 1890s. Emma Richardson, a widow and landlady, is looking through a window. Sam Pipe (son of the basket maker), who became the licensee in 1912, is standing in the doorway. Seven men are smoking pipes, several have walking sticks, two of which are very smart; all of them are wearing bowler hats or caps. Note the boy in the centre with the large watch chain and Eton collar. What is the occasion? Obviously it is the reason for the photograph. The sticks suggest walking, but if so that was to follow; see how their boots shine. In those days the roads were either muddy or dusty.

The Basket Maker's Shop, Grundisburgh, *c.* 1900. John Wilgrass Pipe was making baskets and sieves here in 1843; he was also a cooper. Kebble Wilgrave Pipe was basket maker and cooper in 1881, and employed ten men and three boys. The withies (or osiers) were grown in the district. Most basket makers had their own withy beds. Moist ground was most suitable for growing withies, which were planted in the winter and took three years to reach maturity. The baskets, used for many purposes both locally and much further away, were made in all shapes and sizes. In 1874 there were over forty basket makers in Suffolk. The cooper also made a wide range of containers: large barrels, casks, small barrels to carry beer to the fields, barrels for butter churns, wooden pails for milking and carrying water, and so on. In the photograph a load of withies has just arrived. Usually, it is small boys who get in front for the camera, but here they appear shy and are standing well back. Instead the little girls, all wearing fur tippets, have lined up in front. Eventually the cottage shown here became dilapidated before it was listed as a Grade Two building. Attempts were made to repair it, but each attempt only revealed how bad its state had become. A new cottage in the same style was built on the site and is known as Basket Maker's Cottage.

Seckford Hall, Great Bealings, 1855. The home of Thomas Seckford, the Woodbridge benefactor who also paid for the first set of county maps done by Saxon. At the beginning of this century the Hall was in a state of decay and deserted, but in the late 1940s it was rescued by Sir Ralph Harwood and turned into a hotel.

Boulge Hall, demolished in 1956. The Fitzgerald family came to live here around 1835, but Edward Fitzgerald went to live in a cottage which stood in the grounds. He once called Boulge 'one of the dullest places in England'.

The Mansion, Easton, *c.* 1911. This was the Suffolk seat of the Duke of Hamilton who also had three seats in Scotland and only occasionally resided at Easton. In 1920 the Mansion was taken down piecemeal, shipped to America, and rebuilt.

The Red Lion, Martlesham, pre-1940. A sixteenth-century building with a fine Charles II bow window. Note the figurehead under the eaves. At the Battle of Sole Bay in 1672, the Dutch Fleet consisted of 180 ships and the Allied Fleet had 156 ships. Towards the end of the battle the Dutch ship *Stavoren* was disabled and captured by the *Cambridge*. It is said that this sign at the Red Lion was the figurehead from the *Stavoren*. The sign is the reason for the local expression 'as red as Martlesham Lion'.

The Deben Foreshore and Sailing Club, Waldringfield, 1946. The parish has 904 acres of land and 190 acres of tidal river, salt marsh and foreshore. It is given as 'Walringafelda' in Domesday . 'The overflowing river, flashing blue and silver in the sunlight, winds its way towards the sea. Saltines and mudflats . . . sweep along the channel verge.' (Revd A.N.H. Waller, Rector of Waldringfield).

Bungalows by the Deben at Waldringfield, early 1930s. The first two were built by a Mr Stollery.

Waldringfield Regatta Week, 1958. In 1921 eleven enthusiasts met in a beach hut on the Foreshore; that meeting was the beginning of the Waldringfield Sailing Club. Nine years later it had thirty members, today it has over six hundred.

Waldringfield Beach, 1913. Carting shingle from the beach. Today, Suffolk Horses have gone and there is hardly any shingle left. The carts, commonly called dung carts or tumbrils, could be tipped to release these loads. The front horses were in traces to assist the horses in shafts because the loads would have been very heavy.

Coprolite washing by the Deben, Waldringfield, 1880s. Coprolite is the fossilized remains of prehistoric animals and dung. Its first recorded use as manure was in 1717, but it wasn't until the middle of the nineteenth century that its great value as phosphate fertilizer was fully realized. The first coprolite mill was at Snape in 1843 and the first diggings in the Woodbridge area began in 1845. From 1860 to 1890 it was a flourishing industry. In the 1870s 10,000 tons were being sent annually from quays on the Deben and Orwell to factories in Ipswich. The pits, all dug by hand, were as much as twenty to thirty feet deep. Land owners leased digging rights to contractors and local men found digging coprolite a better paid job than farm work: they were paid 4¹/₂d. per cubic yard and the coprolite fetched up to £2 10s. per ton. First the top soil was removed and put aside and then a trench was dug to get at the coprolite. This process was repeated and the earlier trench filled in. As the land was restored little evidence of the diggings remained except a few hollows here and there. A large quantity of crag had to be removed and sifted to get a quantity of coprolite which was taken by horse and cart to the washer.

The May Bush Inn and the Deben, Waldringfield in the early twentieth century, reputed to have been a smugglers' inn. In the fields near here quantities as large as a thousand tons of coprolite were dug. After sifting, washing and sorting it was loaded on to barges and taken to Ipswich to Fison's and Packard's factory to be ground and turned into phosphate fertilizers.

Old tree stump on Waldringfield Heath, c. 1920. The exposed roots show how much soil has been blown away.

Waldringfield church. There has been a church on this site for seven hundred years. In 1841 a burial urn dating from Saxon times was dug up from the churchyard, which suggests it had been a burial ground in pre-Christian days. At least two centenarians are buried in the churchyard. A tithe barn once stood on the north side of the church. Members of the Waldringfield family of Waller have been rectors here in unbroken succession, father to son, since 1862, and the Revd Charles Waller was the rector from 1833–8. A Waldringfield church memorandum of 1873, when the Revd Thomas Henry Waller was rector, says: 'A man may pursue his worldly work at one hour and be upon his knees in God's House at another on the same day . . . Again, there is no inconsistency or impropriety in coming to Church in a working dress. Let a man, if the occasion require it, go straight from the plough and say his prayers in the congregation, and the soil upon his clothes . . . Far more pleasing to God . . . than young men and maidens whose only object at a Sunday service seems to be to lounge or sleep or laugh or display a gay dress. . .' In 1873 Coal and Clothing Clubs were 'open to all needy parishioners subject to the approval of honorary members subscribing ten shillings or upwards a year. The Clothing must consist of under garments or materials for bedding; not of bonnets, caps, ribbons or outside finery. Benefit members are required to pay their pence every fortnight . . .'

The Baptist Chapel on Waldringfield Heath, 1920. The chapel is still open but has no resident pastor today. Suffolk has a tradition of Nonconformity; in 1698 Celia Fiennes recorded: 'Thence I went to Woodbridge seven mile, mostly lanes enclosed countrys; this is a little market town but has a great meeting for the Dessenters [sic].'

The Street, Waldringfield, *c.* 1891. In late medieval times the village had a clothing industry.

Waldringfield in 1897, showing the cement works on the right. Waldringfield Cement Works was opened in 1872. The cement was made from river mud chalk. On the ebb tide a barge dropped down the river. The barge would be run ashore and a couple of men throw twenty-five tons of mud into it in less than five hours. The mud was taken to the factory, mixed with chalk, washed, and put into pits for about four weeks. Then it was put into kilns, of which there were twelve, with layers of coke and coal and burned. Later it was taken out and ground, bagged, and loaded into barges for dispatch. Balls in the crushing mill weighing 30 cwt reduced the cement clinker to powder, and produced a great deal of dust and noise in the neighbourhood during the process. The works closed in 1907 and moved to Claydon.

The post office, Waldringfield, *c*. 1904. The Waldringfield post office has moved several times. An older photograph, too delicate to reproduce, shows an earlier post office more picturesque and hidden among a profusion of flowers.

Waldringfield, *c*. 1900. A group of children 'up the road'. Possibly they are returning from school, or is it an outing? Note how smartly they are dressed. There is a second group further back, in which the girls appear to have sunshades (a holiday?), and one very small figure all alone. It is summer, but there is smoke from some chimneys as fires were needed for cooking in 1900.

The Old Rectory at Hemley in 1919, now much rebuilt. Count von di Schulenburg lived here in around 1910. He entertained naval and military personnel from abroad and was said to have made many nightly excursions to places along the coast. He was suspected of being a German spy.

Newbourne Fox. Crowds came to the Fox from over a wide area on Whit Wednesdays to dance and frolic and to bowl for a copper kettle.

Newbourne Hall, the home of the artist Stuart Somerville. Newbourne was subjected to change in 1934 when a Land Settlement Association estate was established in the parish. The LSA was a limited company, partially backed by the Government, which settled unemployed industrial workers on the land. Houses were built for the tenants who were each provided with about five acres of land, pig houses, outbuildings and a large greenhouse, together with an organization for marketing their produce. The Newbourne estate was one of several established throughout the country. During the 1980s the Association was wound up and the holdings were sold. Newbourne was noted for its giants, the brothers George and Meadows Page, both of whom were 7ft 7in tall. George toured the country and was exhibited at sideshows; he died in 1870 and is buried in the churchyard at Newbourne.

Waldringfield Cliff and Foreshore, 1880. This photograph was taken on a glass plate by Mr Thomas Naunton Waller (cousin to the then rector, the Revd T.H. Waller). He was a keen photographer and took many photographs during the 1880s, but he got tired of having to take the lens cap off the camera every time he took a photograph, so he invented a mechanical device for the removal of the cap. He told Kodak or Eastman of his invention and it is believed that his idea was adopted. It is probable that this is one of the first photographs taken by a camera with an automatic shutter. More of his photographs appear later, and so do members of the Waller family.

Ufford and Eyke to Snape, Orford and Bawdsey

The moving Finger writes; and, having writ, Moves on.
Edward Fitzgerald

Ufford Ford and Bridge, at the Deben, early 1900s. Ufford takes its name from Uffa, a Scandinavian invader. The Venerable Bede mentions a ford between Rendlesham and Eyke (there were three fords at Ufford). The Revd Richard Luskin (or Lovekin) was rector here in 1621. His parishioners complained that he was 'a very cold preacher and a common swearer'. In 1641 there was a petition to have him removed but he remained rector until 1678 when he died at the age of 110 years, having taken the previous Sunday's service as usual – or so the story has it.

Ufford church, *c.* 1905. The font cover in the church has been described as 'the most beautiful in the world'. When William Dowsing came to Ufford in 1648 on his destructive tour of churches he was prevented from entering the church for two hours. The beauty of the font cover stayed even his hand and he ordered that the cover should be spared. Dowsing, who was a Laxfield man, was appointed Parliamentary Visitor for Cambridge and Suffolk and told to remove everything in churches remotely savouring of 'popery'. In his tour of vandalism he visited about fifty churches. Grundisburgh was one that was spared. In 1773, Thomas Crisp of Ufford advertised his Suffolk stallion 'at a fee of eight shillings as a sire to get good stock'. All the Suffolk Horses in the male line in the *Stud Book* are descended from this horse foaled in 1768.

The Street, Eyke, *c.* 1900. 'Eyke' is either Scandinavian or Dutch, or derived from 'oak'. The two men by the horse and trap seem interested in something down the street, while the group beyond seem interested by the camera. A horse and gig stand on the left by the thatched house.

The Street, Eyke, *c.* 1912. The same viewpoint, but this time a motor car stands by the Elephant and Castle, which dates from 1650. In 1707, when John and Thomas Fuller took over the old Castle Inn, their father converted a house 'at the corner of the lane' into an inn and called it the Elephant and Castle. 'Ringing the Bull' was played here. One of the oldest pub games, it involves swinging a bull ring suspended from the ceiling on to a hook on the wall.

Eyke School and school house, 1960. When it opened on Monday 14 June 1857 the fee was one penny per week per pupil, but it was later raised to three pennies per week or one shilling per quarter to be paid in advance. Schooling became free at the end of the century.

Where the bomb fell at Eyke on a moonlit night in June 1940. The aeroplane got caught in a tree and crashed. That weekend the place was crowded with sightseers. The site is the old Rectory garden. This is believed to have been the first, or one of the first bombs to have been dropped on Suffolk in the Second World War.

Eyke, 1900s. In 1350 the parishioners of Eyke attacked the Rectory, broke down the gates, burst open a chest, and took away some of the contents, the property of Robert de Redenhale who was also Lord of the Manor. In 1587 the parishioners revolted again, this time against Thomas Seckford, who had threatened to fine them if they persisted in wearing the German felt hats on Sundays and festivals instead of English pile hats. The parishioners, who refused to comply with Seckford's orders, were fined by the courts in 1589 and the following two years. Dowsing visited Eyke church in January 1650 and broke down 'twenty-five superstitious Pictures and took up a Superstitious Inscription'. Before the windmill there had been a watermill here, on the Deben. The Revd J.G. Darling, who died in 1891, had, during his time as incumbent, repaired the very dilapidated church and built a new school and rectory.

'The dear little cottage' on the road to Ufford, pre-1914. This was the home of the Reeve or Bailiff of the Manor and the subject of Chancery proceedings in 1466 and 1471. It is now Reeve Hall, a much grander establishment. In the intervening period it was turned into two cottages, then fell into disrepair and was condemned.

Snape village, *c*. 1900.

The Crown Inn, Snape flooded by the River Alde nearly half a mile away in 1952. Floods occurred regularly, and men who worked at the Maltings had then to go round by Abbey Farm to get to work which took them half an hour. The Golden Key, just round the corner, also got flooded.

The Plough Inn and Bridge, Snape. Close to the inn is the Maltings, which employed two hundred men; it ceased production in 1965 and has been converted into an Opera House. In 1846 Garrett Newson was shipping from Snape 'annually to the Port of London and other markets, two hundred thousand quarters of barley and nine hundred quarters of malt in vessels from sixty to ninety tons burthen.' A quarter of barley weighed 4cwt.

Snape post office.

The Crown at a later date. This fifteenth-century building was once used by smugglers. One room is called the 'Old Codgers' Room' because at a time when this room was without any glass in the window the elderly habitués refused to move although a bitter northeast wind was blowing. The panelling in the inn was fitted in 1991 and came from the Dorchester Hotel, London.

The Market Hill, Orford. In the centre is the fortified keep of Orford Castle (built in 1165). From here the house where Margaret Catchpole (see p. 92) was captured after her escape from Ipswich gaol in 1800 can be seen. The castle was built by Henry II to guard Orford Haven. Orford was once a busy port; in 1359 it sent three warships and sixty-two men to assist in the Siege of Calais. There used to be a market every Monday, two annual fairs and a yearly Court of Sessions. Until the Reform Act of 1832, Orford returned two Members of Parliament. It also had the Wild Man. According to legend, fishermen caught this strange creature which was half-man and half-dog and covered with red hair. They took him to the governor of the castle who got experts to examine him. He was only capable of guttural sounds and refused to wear clothes. A room was provided for him at the castle where he would sit close to the fire, holding his head in his hands. One night he escaped, fishermen saw him plunging into the sea, and after that he was never seen again. Another version has it that his body was covered in fish scales, that he was tortured in the castle to try and make him speak, and that after his escape he returned to Orford.

On the left, just past the figure, is the Crown and Castle, where Robert Watson Watt stayed while conducting his early experimental work on radar at the Ness. He visited the Jolly Sailor Inn and thought its beer was like 'nectar and ambrosia' – it still is.

The Butley and Orford Oysterage, Market Hill, Orford. Note the sign, which should need no explanation. This has been at various times a bicycle shop, an electricians and a greengrocers shop. Happily for lovers of good food, especially oysters, smoked salmon and other smoked fish, simply and pleasantly served, it is still a restaurant.

Richard Pinney cutting rushes in the Deben, 1948. A bolt (bundle) of the rushes weighed 60lb when green but only 10lb when dried. Richard Pinney hired an old warehouse on Orford Quay and stocked it up with rushes, and hired a room in Market Hill (above the later restaurant run by Mrs Pinney) where the rush products were made. When the rush business expanded it was moved to more spacious premises at Debenham.

The big freeze of 1962/3, when the Orford river was filled with blocks of ice.

Orford Quay, 1953. This thresher shark, caught by Richard Pinney and Ted Hawes, was 15ft in length, its 7ft tail like a broad sword. It was almost as long as the dinghy from which it had been netted. After 'pulling their guts out', the two men dragged it to the shallows with only a single strand of netting remaining over its snout. With a twelve bore gun it was then shot in the mouth at point blank range. It was the biggest thresher shark caught on this coast since 1877. Thresher sharks hunt in packs, using their tails to thresh the water to drive their quarry – usually mackerel or herring – into a concentration.

Oyster Pits, 1958. Unloading Portuguese oysters (the cane baskets are also from Portugal). Butley Creek is a salt water tributary of the River Ore. Butley Creek had had an oyster fishery at one time, and a few of the Natives still existed despite all the neglect when Richard Pinney came to Orford and had bacon and oyster breakfasts at the Crown and Castle. His ambition was to restore Orford's reputation for oysters. The Native has a closed season, but the Portuguese is edible all the year round. As the Portuguese will not release their eggs in low temperature waters, however, they are transplanted into Butley Creek. Tom Brinkley warned Richard Pinney, 'If you want to lose your money, do you put it into oysters.' Yet, in spite of difficulties, mainly over importing, the Portuguese flourished in the unpolluted waters of Butley Creek, as a visit to the restaurant in Market Hill will prove.

The 'octopus', used for an even distribution of oysters.

Dredging oysters, Butley Creek, 1965. Left to right: John Thacker, Richard Pinney, Steve Richardson. Richard Pinney began to sell oysters on a commercial scale in 1960; at that time he had about one and a half million Portuguese oysters. He was then importing them every year to keep up his supply.

Oyster dredging, Butley Creek, 1965. Left to right: Steve Richardson, Richard Pinney, John Pinney, John Thacker. The ice blocks of the severe winter of 1962/3 had taken the embedded oysters off in the tide. Most of them died.

Oyster Pit, Butley Creek, 1965. John Pinney and John Thacker unloading dredged oysters.

Sudbourne Hall, built around 1800 but now demolished, was noted for its shooting parties; the Prince of Wales (later Edward VII) was a frequent visitor. Kenneth Clark, who became Director of the National Gallery and Chairman of the Arts Council, spent his boyhood years here. During the Second World War the estate was requisitioned by the War Department and used for tank training. The village was evacuated.

Billy King mowing the polo ground at Chillesford Lodge in 1936. The mowing machine was made by Ransomes, Sims and Jefferies of Ipswich and is still in good working order today.

Alderton. The Street in the early 1900s.

The Bawdsey Star, a sixteenth-century building.

The Street, Bawdsey, *c.* 1900.

East Lane, Bawdsey, *c.* 1940.

Ferry Road, Bawdsey. The Revd Allot Tighe-Gregory was appointed by the Bishop of Norwich in 1845 to 'the most neglected parish in the diocese', and remained the vicar of Bawdsey until 1910. Among other things he established a school at Bawdsey around 1853. In the church is a tablet to Edward and Edith Cavell of Bawdsey Hall, forebears of Nurse Edith Cavell who was shot at Brussels during the First World War.

The old school at Bawdsey. Unfortunately, the school at Bawdsey backed on to the sewer and epidemics were rife until a new school was built on another site. From school records: 'It is impossible to ventilate the school without causing mischief to occupants.' 'Unless I can get some fuel it will be impossible to keep the school open.'

Bawdsey Ferry. Prior to 1730 a Robert Hamblin was the ferry boatman. About 1895 Sir Cuthbert Quilter installed a steam ferry operated on chains across the river. It had two boats (*Lady Beatrice* and *Lady Quilter*) and they were large enough to take a coach and four horses.

Bawdsey Ferry seen from the Felixstowe shore. The chain ferry ceased working in 1931. Bawdsey Manor is in the background.

Bawdsey Manor, with the Rockery in the foreground, *c.* 1920. Cuthbert Quilter started building this manor around 1873. From time to time he added another tower until there was a total of nine towers. His indoor staff included a butler, footman, valet, hall boy, a cook, three kitchen staff and six housemaids. There were fourteen gardeners and five gamekeepers. The Kaiser is said to have stopped at the Manor before the First World War. Cuthbert Quilter is said to have bought *The Scandal*, Edward Fitzgerald's yacht, and renamed it *The Sapphire*. A millionaire (partner in a firm of accountants and a director of the National Telephone Company), he spent twenty years and a fortune building and adding to his manor. He died in 1911 and was taken on a wagon, drawn by four Suffolk Horses, to Bawdsey churchyard. In 1936 the manor was sold to the Air Ministry and Sir Robert Watson-Watt moved from Orford to continue his radar development at Bawdsey Manor.

Seamark on Bawdsey Cliffs, *c.* 1906. In 1686 the sign then on the cliffs was described as 'a pyramid supporting a pole. At right angles . . . a longarm, at the end of which is a brazier.' The sign shown here bore red and white bands and was the leading mark for the channel in the sea by which vessels could proceed to Woodbridge Haven. In 1924 Trinity House announced that the Bawdsey Seamark had been demolished 'in consequence of the erosion of the cliffs. The Seamark will not be replaced.'

Bawdsey Ferry. 'Scroggie' in his boat.

SECTION FIVE

People and Occasions

There are people and people.
Proverb

Woodbridge Horse Show, 1905.

Woodbridge, 1909. Celebration of the centenary of the birth of Edward Fitzgerald.

Woodbridge Regatta day, early 1900s. The Deben Yacht Club, Woodbridge was founded in 1838, which makes it one of the oldest yacht clubs in the country. The first regatta was held on 8 September 1838; in the following September the crowd at the Regatta numbered 'not less than five thousand persons assembled'. There were two sailing races for small yachts, rowing matches for four-oared galleys, four-oared ship's boats and two-oared boats, and a duck hunt. In the evening there was a firework display and a dinner at the Anchor Inn. Edward Fitzgerald, who was a member, did not enter his yacht in 1869 and wrote to a friend, 'I would not muddle with the Regatta.'

Wickham Market Bowls Club, 1897.

Waldringfield Deben Week. The first regatta was held in 1906 and another in 1909. The Sailing Club was not founded until 1921. In 1937 the club was affiliated to the Yacht Racing Association. By the time of the 1951 regatta, over 600 entries were recorded, compared with the five boats that raced in the early days of the club.

Sporting schoolboys, Snape, 1930s.

Disembarking from Bawdsey Ferry.

Polo at Chillesford Lodge in the late 1930s.

Polo spectators at Chillesford Lodge in the late 1930s.

George Snowden at Chillesford in the 1930s, wearing his working clothes and his chapel clothes.

Blaxhall Ship, 1946. The occasion is a supper for returned POWs. The vicar is by the oil lamp, note the man in uniform and the Union Jack. Sheep used to be shorn in the pub's yard and as 'ship' is dialect for sheep the pub may once have been known as The Sheep. Sheep were brought from a wide district to be shorn here and the shearing was done by a group called the Blaxhall Company of Sheep Shearers, which may have originated as far back as the sixteenth century. The Blaxhall Ship was known for its traditional folk songs. Step-dancing was also practised here – improvised stepping to the music of an accordion. Largesse Spending, Harvest Frolics or Suppers, Horkeys are all different names for celebrating after harvest. The Big Room has also been used for coroner's inquests and weddings, by the Tithe Commissioners and the Parish Council. George Ewart Evans, the author of many books on rural life and work, traditions and superstitions, the lore of horses and horsemen and a pioneer of oral history, lived at Blaxhall for a time – his wife was headmistress at the school. His book, *Ask the Fellows who Cut the Hay*, is mainly about Blaxhall.

Pantomime at Martlesham, *c*. 1930s.

Procession at Burgh, *c*. 1910, with the band in the front.

The village orchestra at Waldringfield, just after the First World War.

Dancing round the maypole at Snape, 1930s. This was taken in a meadow near Hall Farm belonging to Sir Guy Hamblin of Yoxford, owner of the well known Yoxford herd of Red Polls.

Margaret Catchpole was born at Hoo in 1762, lived at Nacton and went to work in the house of the Ipswich brewer, John Cobbold. She stole a horse, apparently to meet her lover Will Laud who was a smuggler, was apprehended, brought to trial, and sentenced to death in August 1797. She was reprieved, the sentence was commuted to seven years transportation and she was sent to Ipswich gaol. She escaped from gaol, was recaptured, condemned to death again, and was again reprieved and transported. She died in Australia in 1819. The Revd Richard Cobbold, son of John Cobbold, wrote a novel based on her life entitled *The History of Margaret Catchpole, a Suffolk Girl*, first published in 1845. This illustration is from the book and probably bears little resemblance to the real woman, the handbills for the arrest (no doubt prejudiced) described her as a hard-featured woman.

Waldringfield Cricket Club, 1923. The Club existed in 1888, but at some point it became dormant and was later revived.

Snape football team, 1941/2. Some of those pictured include, back row, left to right: G. Davidson (trainer), two soldiers in the district, E. Bastowe, G. Howe (village PC). Front row: T. Mayhew, R. Goodchild, D. Davidson, B. Howe, R. Wright (captain).

Sunday school treat at Grundisburgh, *c.* 1900.

Group at Butley Chapel, *c.* 1895.

A garden meeting at Waldringfield, July 1956. The speaker is S. Shunn, head gardener at Chantry Park, Ipswich.

The men who built Rendlesham Hall, 1899. (Some records say it was rebuilt in 1871.) It was demolished soon after the Second World War. Redwold, the first East Anglian king to become a Christian, held his court at Rendlesham. His wife remained a Pagan, however, and eventually she persuaded him to return to Paganism.

The men who delivered the mail. Postmen outside Woodbridge post office, *c*. 1909.

A wedding at Grundisburgh.

A Snape man marries an Aldeburgh girl. The wedding of Bob and Doris Ling on 12 April 1941. Bob Ling worked at Snape Maltings and was married immediately before he went into the Navy. This photograph was taken outside the bride's home. The brick wall in front of window was a 'blast wall', providing protection against bombing.

The Golden Wedding of the Revd T. Waller and Jane Waller, Waldringfield, 1906. Back row: Mary Waller, Arthur Waller, Annie Waller, John Waller, Violet Waller, left to right: Dr Alfred Waller, Agnes Waller, Tom Waller, Kate Waller. Middle row: Connie Waller, Trevor, Tommy Waller, Jane and Thomas Waller, Beth, Nellie Waller, Janet. Front row: Jack, Gwen, Cyril. The Revd T.H. Waller was rector of Waldringfield from 1862 to 1906. The family has flourished on both sides of the Deben for centuries. In 1428 a William Waller was Lord of the Manor of Peyton Hall at Ramsholt. The linking with Waldringfield is recorded in 1639 when Jeptha Waller married Susan Goss of Waldringfield. Since the Revd Thomas Waller became rector of Waldringfield in 1862 his descendants and their spouses have been landowners, bankers, engineers, doctors, nurses, publishers, or rectors of Waldringfield.

A family group at Martlesham.

Mother and children at Snape in the late 1920s. Note the cloche hats.

Father and daughter, Martlesham, 1927.
Arthur Hill and Flo.

Girl with perambulator, Martlesham,
1912.

Grandfather, grandmother and granddaughter,
1919. Samuel and Emma Ling at home, High
Terrace, Blaxhall. Samuel Ling was a maltster
and in the summer he used to shear sheep (see
p. 89). When Mr Ling was born at Blaxhall,
most of the families there bore the name Ling
or Smith and had biblical Christian names such
as Esau, Elijah or Aaron.

Swimming in the river by Snape Bridge, 1930s. This hump bridge was built in 1802, it was demolished in 1959, the first victim of Sizewell atomic power station, according to Norman Scarfe.

Pettistree Women's Institute off to Clacton, in 1926. The Women's Institute movement originated in Canada and came to Britain in 1915. The Pettistree Women's Institute was founded in 1918 with a membership of over thirty. The early meetings were held in the Church Room but within ten years the Institute had built and paid for its own hall.

Waldringfield Women's Institute in 1949. Waldringfield Women's Institute was founded in 1924. This shows its twenty-fifth birthday celebration. Mrs Sutton is handing a bouquet to Lady Albermarle. Miss G. Waller was the President.

Martlesham Women's Institute in the 1960s. It looks like another birthday party.

Greyhound assembly, *c.* 1911. The exact location is unidentified, but it is thought to be somewhere at Wickham Market.

Waldringfield Regatta, 1924. The Thames barge *Dover Castle* is run on to the beach and used by the committee. Her rotting timbers now lie in the river mud near Woodbridge. The large yacht (centre) is the *Elf*, the fastest yacht in the fleet.

A picnic on Waldringfield Heath, 1924. Waldringfield had many occasions recorded by photographs which have been carefully preserved. For this we must thank that keen photographer, Thomas Naunton Waller, and those who have followed him, for the Waller collection of photographs, and the Waldringfield people who have realized the value of this photographic record.

A double wedding at Bawdsey, 1938: Russell Walker and Yvonne Shelcott; Ernie Kallmeier and Ivy Shelcott.

Waldringfield, 1900s. When the harvest was done there was a Harvest Frolic in the schoolroom, complete with a baron of beef, potatoes, fruit and custard, and a barrel of beer in the corner. There was dancing to an accordion. Next day there was an outing to Ipswich in this farm wagon. The wagon has two sets of shafts and was known as a 'double-breaster'. Their lives must have been arduous and not without worries but it was a settled world, a world within a world, when a trip to Ipswich was a day to be remembered. The next decade shattered that world.

Waldringfield, 1914. These young men are off to join Kitchener's Army. Some of those in the photograph are: E. Moules, N. Scoggins, J. Stebbings. The settled rural world begins to fall apart.

Recruits at Orford during the First World War. The Castle keep is in the background.

Steve Harper of the Jolly Sailor, Orford, 1930s. He was landlord from January 1914 until his death in May 1939. Among other things he was noted for his dazzling waistcoats, his fund of stories, and the introduction of 'stout and oyster evenings' at the inn. His portrait was painted by T.C. Dugdale and hung in the Royal Academy. The Jolly Sailor is a seventeenth-century building with a front of a later period, and was once the haunt of smugglers. The Little Dogs of Orford can still be seen at the inn, none much bigger than a large mouse. It is thought that they are 'muff dogs' brought from China by an Orford sailor two or three centuries ago.

Mr Pipe, the last of the Pipe family, basket makers of Grundisburgh.

Bawdsey Women's Institute outing. The hats are a guide to the date: late 1920s or early 1930s.

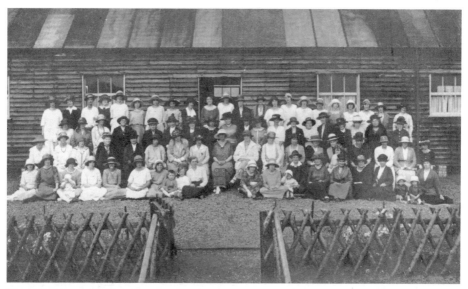

The Bawdsey and Alderton Women's Institute outside their Hall. The Hall was opened on 24 November 1922 and each year afterwards a party was held on the anniversary day. Lady Quilter is sitting in the middle of the front row. The WI split in the 1960s. The Hall was also used by the Boys Brigade and later by the local cubs, by which time the hall was called the Black Hut.

Pettistree Women's Institute outing to Yarmouth, 1920.

The Crisp family at Playford Hall, *c*. 1895. The name Crisp will always be associated with the Suffolk Horse (see p. 63). Shown here are Mrs Crisp, the three Misses Crisp and George Crisp.

Bawdsey Home Guard with a 6-in naval gun at Bawdsey Beach during the Second World War.

'Scroggie' and Albert Ramsby, Bawdsey. 'Scroggie' (Mr Hunt) was an old sailor, though not a native of Bawdsey, who used to sail in windjammers to Australia. He worked for Raymond Quilter, and managed to walk to the ferry where he mended nets. Albert Ramsby was a cowman at Bawdsey.

George Johnson and young relations at Wickham Market. George Johnson, who died in 1945, had been the Wickham gravedigger. On the sign of the house may be seen the sign-board of F.J. Johnson, the builder. The house has since been demolished.

Mr Sutton driving his motor car, an 8hp Darracq, in 1904. Mr Sutton and his wife taught at Waldringfield School from 1897 to 1932.

Thomas Churchyard and his daughter Laura at home in Cumberland Street, Woodbridge, *c.* 1860. Thomas Churchyard was an artist, a Quaker and a lawyer. He was one of a group with Edward Fitzgerald, Bernard Barton, the Revd George Crabbe (son of the poet) and W.B. Donne known as the Wits of Woodbridge who met at The Bull Inn. In 1892 Edward Clodd of Aldeburgh founded the Omar Khayyam Club which also met at the Bull, Woodbridge.

Martello Tower at Bawdsey with Mr and Mrs Shelcott and an uncle. The Martello towers were erected in the 1800s as a defence against invasion by Napoleon. Twenty years later William Cobbett called them 'ridiculous things' and 'incessant sinks of money'.

Herbert Shelcott with one of the Quilter Ponies.

Raymond Quilter and his aeroplane. Sir Raymond Quilter (1902–59) was a grandson of the first Sir Cuthbert Quilter. His aeroplane was reputed to be the best radio-equipped private aeroplane in the country. When parachuting was still in its infancy he used to make daring parachute jumps to thrill visitors at Felixstowe. Roger Quilter, the composer, was the son of the first Sir Cuthbert Quilter.

Gardeners and the bothy at Bawdsey Manor.

Jubilee celebrations at Waldringfield, 1887. Old Mrs Moules is centre. There is a good line-up of fine wheelbarrows, ready no doubt for a wheelbarrow race. The cause for the occasion was, of course, Queen Victoria's Golden Jubilee. This is another photograph taken by Thomas Naunton Waller.

Education

Our minds want clothes as much as our bodies.
Samuel Butler

Waldringfield School, 1910.

Waldringfield School, 1927. Back row, left to right: Rose Nunn, Elsie Wicks, Ruby Bear, Ethel Bead, Gert Read, Miriam Dickson, Vera Brown, Phyllis Dickerson. Second row, from second left: Vera Bear, Mabel Read, Fred Wicks, Grace Garham. Front row, from sixth left: Terry Stevens, Bob Stevens, Walter Alexander, Bill Dickerson, and Sylvia Spooner.

Hoo School, *c*. 1900.

Little Bealings School, *c*. 1920.

Little Bealings School, *c.* 1928.

Woodbridge School, 1924.

Eyke School, 1927.

Gardening at Eyke School.

Waldringfield School garden, 1911.

Pedigree breeding pen maintained by the boys of Snape School in the 1930s. The boys built the poultry houses and made all the other apparatus.

Rhode Island pullets reared by the pupils of Snape School in the 1930s. Poultry keeping was just one aspect of rural education at Snape School when Mr Stanley Reeves was head-master.

Some of the pullets raised at Snape School in 1936. The pupils attended to the feeding and the collection and sale of eggs. The book keeping involved made a practical base for arithmetic. Joe Parker and Mary Bye are in the centre.

Group practice at Snape School, 1930s.

Pupils of Snape School learning to dive, 1930s.

Wickham Market School, *c*. 1890.

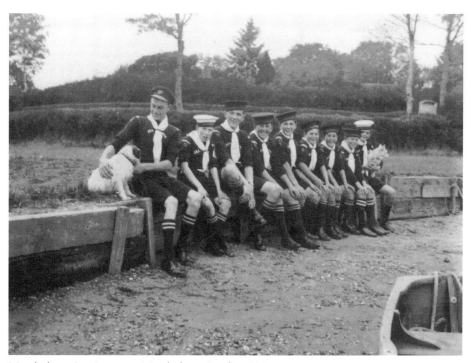

Martlesham Sea Scouts at Martlesham Creek, 1934.

An unidentified school group of the 1900s, thought to be from Woodbridge. The 1870 Education Act required districts without adequate schooling to have school boards, and made school attendance compulsory for all children between five and thirteen years of age, although they could leave at ten years if good progress had been made. A charge of up to ninepence per week could be made for schooling until 1891 when elementary education became free. In the afternoons the boys were taught carpentry and gardening, and the girls were taught sewing.

Bawdsey Sunday school with the Revd Mr Sherlock, 1950.

Agriculture

Husbandry is craftsmanship, the sum of all craftsmanship, and to try to turn it into something else, a business among businesses, is the way to utter disaster.

H.J. Massingham

Agriculture implies so vastly more than the growing of crops . . .

Sir George Stapledon

Ploughing at Waldringfield. Arthur Tuckwell with his horses, Bob and Ruby. An acre per day was the usual rate and this entailed walking about twelve miles. The photograph explains the terms 'land horse' and 'furrow horse'.

Ploughing at Martlesham, late 1920s. The ploughman is Frank Foster, the horses are Suffolks. Almost all the field has been ploughed and he is now going round the outside, ploughing the headland. A man could talk to his horses. A horseman, though not actually owning them, always called them 'his' horses. The horseman was the most important man in the community and had a secret fund of horse lore. (See *Horse Power and Magic* by George Ewart Evans)

Harvesting corn with binder and horses at Bealings. Later, the bound sheaves (right) will be put into stooks, or shocks as they were called in Suffolk. The binder had come into general use by the end of the nineteenth century and remained in use until around 1950 when the combine took its place.

A break for refreshment at harvest, known as 'fourses' or 'beevers', Waldringfield, c. 1900. This was before farming became dehumanized and men could talk and laugh as they worked. The stone jars suggest beer, the bottle cold tea. It was customary for the women to bring the men's refreshment to the field.

Rabbit auction at Waldringfield. The horses which have been pulling the binder are in the background. The rabbits were caught as they tried to escape from the diminishing area of standing corn, and were auctioned at the end of the day to provide funds for the Harvest Frolic or outing. This photograph provides another instance of the community that was once part of farming. 'Oh, more than happy countryman!,' despite the labour of those years.

Billy King drag raking at Chillesford, with Rose, a Suffolk Punch, 1930s. Any remaining loose parts of the crop were carefully raked and gathered in those days. In earlier times it would have been gleaned by local people and eventually ground into flour to make their bread.

Threshing at Bealings. There are two men on top of the threshing machine – one to cut the string bonds of the sheaves, the other to feed the sheaves into the drum; two on the corn stack – one to fork sheaves to the other who pitched them on to the threshing machine; another to attend to the machinery. Altogether nine men were needed for threshing. The horse and tumbril on the left take away the full sacks. The steam engine which drove the threshing machine is just out of the picture but the drive belt can be seen just behind the tumbril.

Steam threshing tackle at Waldringfield, 1915. This was the first threshing set in the district and was owned by Mr John Waller. Left to right: a soldier on leave, Mr Bloomfield, Mr Garnham. The engine, an 1870 model, was made by Garretts of Leiston. Note the wheels made of wood. Steam engines were in general use by the end of the nineteenth century and scenes such as this and the one above lasted until combines came into general use.

Hedge laying at Chillesford in the early twentieth century, a regular winter job until farming became industrialized. Note the men's thick hide gloves and the Suffolk pattern bill hook in one man's hand. Regretfully, they are using 'live stakes' – part of the living hedge – instead of stakes cut especially for the purpose. The spade was used to throw the ditch cleanings to the base of the newly laid hedge.

Mr Bretts cleaning roots at Waldringfield. Note his leather leggings and hob-nailed boots. Soil adhering to the roots was removed by knife before the roots were fed to the cattle or sheep. The roots would probably be pulped by a hand-turned machine.

William Chilvers and his son, Reg Chilvers, both thatchers, cutting reed for thatching at the Fleet, Chillesford Lodge in 1956. The third man is unidentified. There is a drainage mill in the background. Reeds were the best and most durable material for thatching.

Annual inspection of the wall, *c.* 1930s. Left to right: Dod Malster (head wallman), Hubert Cordle and Tom Arkle (farmers), and J. Gibb (agent at Chillesford Lodge). Tidal walls had been kept in repair along this part of the coast for hundreds of years. Sheep used to graze them and it has been said that their constant grazing and treading helped to keep the turf and the walls firm – the pounding of their feet filling in any rabbit or rat holes that may appear, and that since the sheep have gone the walls have become weaker.

Poultry at Waldringfield, once a common sight but now a rare one. Most people would agree that free range poultry produce eggs superior to those obtained by intensive methods, but today profit comes before quality.

Prince with small cart at Eyke.

Butter making competition at Wickham Market, *c.* 1910. 'For quantity and quality this country doth exist.' said William Camden of Suffolk butter. And the Suffolk-born Robert Bloomfield wrote: 'Slow rolls the churn; its load of clogging cream At once foregoes its quality and name; From knotty particles first floating wide Congealing butter's dashed from side to side.'

Dick Smyth at Blaxhall with a Friesian bull, an alien breed which ousted the native Red Polls around 1930. The farmer he worked for was a Scotsman.

Game cart at Chillesford Lodge, 1936 (now on loan to the Museum of Rural Life at Stowmarket). The game cart was built around 1912. The interior was fitted with slotted bars, on which pheasants were hung by the neck, and rounded rods, to take hares by the hind legs.

L. Backhouse, gamekeeper and rabbit catcher at Chillesford Lodge, c. 1930.

Woodbridge Horse Show, 1931. Sir Cuthbert Quilter's group of prize-winning Suffolk mares. Bawdsey Porcelain was 1st and Champion, Bawdsey Two-Step took 1st prize. The Woodbridge Horse Show was started in 1871, and has always had close links with the Suffolk Horse Society whose offices have always been in Woodbridge. The first site was at Fair Field, Woodbridge. Its purpose was to encourage horse breeding and at its first show there were Suffolk stallions only; later, Hackneys and coaching stallions were included. It now incorporates the Suffolk Horse Society's Spring Stallion Show. It is the first exhibition of the Suffolk Horse Season. Originally it was held during the third week in March; the stallions could then be seen and judged before they started travelling. (During the mating season stallions travelled the district in order to serve mares.) But in 1901 the show moved to Easter Monday in order to encourage attendance by the general public, and in 1980 it moved to the May Day Bank Holiday. Before the tractor came into general use the Suffolk Horse dominated Suffolk farms. The clean legs (absence of long hair) and superior stamina and pulling power were some of the attributes which made it so popular. The Suffolk Horse Society, founded in 1878, is the oldest heavy horse society and claims that the Suffolk Punch is the oldest breed of heavy horse in the world. The breed almost became extinct in the 1960s but now commands a keen interest.

Haymaking at Pettistree, 1928. 'A faire field full of folke' and horses. The ricks are being built simultaneously. The loose hay is gathered from the windrows and taken to the base of the ricks by horse-drawn sweeps. The tall poles are for the grabs which lift the hay on to the ricks. The horse near the centre is being used to hoist a grab. (On some farms elevators powered by horses were used, the horse plodding round and round to work the elevator.)

Red Polls at Grundisburgh, *c.* 1950. Left to right: C. Ashkettle (head herdsman), Lord Cranworth, F. Last, D. Pendle, W. Ottaway. The cows here all bred by Lord Cranworth, and were heavy milkers and prize winners. They are, left to right: Grundisburgh Morning Glory, Grundisburgh Plumpudding, Grundisburgh Ration, Grundisburgh Chanticleer, Grundisburgh Penguin, Grundisburgh Unexpected. The Grundisburgh herd was founded in 1903 and produced many prize winners and some outstanding bulls such as Grundisburgh Wenceslas and Grundisburgh Paddy. Lord Cranworth was President of the Red Poll Cattle Society in 1907, 1934 and 1950. The Red Poll was once the cattle breed of Suffolk as the Suffolk Punch was the horse. The Red Poll Cattle Society was founded in 1888. Red Polls are a dual-purpose breed, the only truly dual-purpose English breed still in existence. The breed is noted for its ability to produce milk and beef, its longevity, thriftiness, docility and its natural polled characteristic. To see a Red Poll herd – now rare – is to see beauty and utility combined, but once farming ceased to be husbandry and became industry few valued such a combination.

At the back of Martlesham Red Lion, *c*. 1920. The landlord also farmed, and these were some of his animals. The centre one is a pure Red Poll – note her 'clean' nose – but the other has a 'black' nose and is probably a crossbred. The one on the left is a Shorthorn, which at that time was the most popular breed in England.

Marshall traction engine made in 1913 being driven by Mr G.W. Holland of Pettistree in 1965.

STILL MORE
MILK
IS NEEDED

Winter production means more milk in the year—more milk when most needed—more milk when it pays you best. It leads to better dairy farming.

The most important steps are:

★ **PLAN YOUR CALVING**

Arrange for more autumn and winter calvings. Bull your heifers in December.

★ **PLAN FOR WINTER FEEDING**

Feeding stuffs from overseas are still short. Dairy farmers should now grow their own, so plan your autumn and spring croppings to make sure of enough for autumn and winter calvers. Ask your War Agricultural Executive Committee for advice.

★ **BETTER BREEDING**

Improve the output of your herd through better breeding. Higher yielding cows give more winter milk.

THE TEST WILL BE SALES OF WINTER MILK PER COW IN YOUR HERD

A Ministry of Agriculture advertisement in the *Woodbridge and Wickham Market Gazette*, October 1944. There was a time when more and more milk was wanted, when milk surpluses and milk quotas were unknown. This is one of a series of advertisements issued by the Ministry of Agriculture during the war; another exhorted farmers to 'Plough Now! By day and by night!' As the Ministry, through its War Agricultural Executive Committees, had complete control over farming, these advertisements were rather unnecessary.

Silage making at Martlesham, 1950s.

Carrying grass to the pit. The buckrake attached to the rear of the tractor collected grass from the swathe, transported and then tipped it in the silage pit.

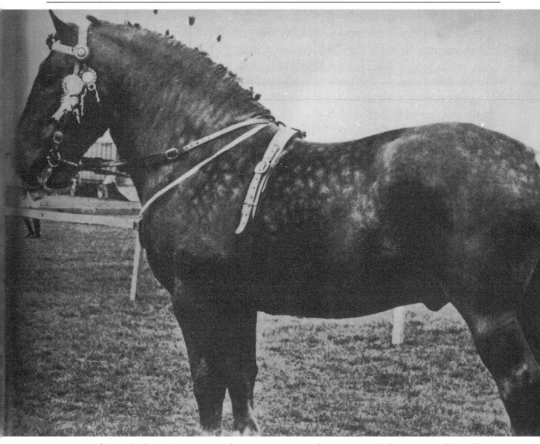

Yeoman of Rowhedge, 8213, second prizewinner in the two- and three-year-old stallions class at the Royal Show in 1953. A Suffolk stallion belonging to the Hollesley Colony Stud. Prize Suffolk Horses were being bred at the Hollesley Estate over 150 years ago, and the tradition continues today. In 1887 the estate became the Colonial College and Training Farms Ltd, and was intended as a training ground for those who wanted to emigrate. The estate was up for sale in 1903 and two years later became the Hollesley Bay Farm Colony, its 'students' 'selected' from the London unemployed – the colonists were paid sixpence a week less stoppages and directed to be of 'prompt obedience', to 'preserve sobriety', and 'observe appointed hours' upon pain of dismissal. In 1938 the estate was conveyed to the Prison Commissioners and became a training borstal for young offenders, some of whom tend, work and show the Suffolk Horses. Brendan Behan, the playwright, is the Colony's most distinguished 'old boy'. The estate now consists of 1,400 acres and has the oldest existing flock of Suffolk Sheep. It has recently completed the Suffolk trinity with the introduction of Red Poll cattle.

The dairy at Bawdsey Manor, pre-1914. This building has been demolished.

Milk men at High House, Bawdsey, with a young helper, complete with white smocks and hats, pails, and three-legged wooden stools for hand milking.

Fred Withers, a gamekeeper for many years on the Bawdsey Estate. The clothes and the gun are what one would expect but the lamb under the arm is unexplained.

Albert Ramsby, milk man at High House, Bawdsey. Note the pigeon holes at the top of the building.

James Shelcot and Bill Cody with horse and steerage hoe at Bawdsey.

Will Clouting driving a four-wheel-drive tractor on the Bawdsey Estate.

Charles Howard, miller.

Charles Howard (right) and George Snowden.

W. Cole, woodman.

F. Kersey, gamekeeper, with ferret. All these men worked on the Chillesford Lodge Estate in the 1930s.

In the Manor Drive, Bawdsey. These Suffolk Horses may have been on their way to a show. The head horseman always took the lead. The horses belonged to Cuthbert Quilter. He was a wealthy man who moved to Suffolk in 1873, became Liberal MP for South Suffolk in 1885, and was made a baronet in 1906. His stud of Suffolk Horses was famous and won many prizes. He also had a pedigree herd of Red Polls and a flock of Suffolk Sheep.

A team of Suffolk Horses hauling a wagon load of corn at Bawdsey. Note the horsemen's hats, smocks and whips and the fine condition of the horses, with the pouch-like objects dangling by their forelegs, a characteristic of the Bawdsey Stud. (Does anyone now know the reason for those 'pouches'?) The wagon, too, is worthy of attention. Wagons which could well be described as 'galleons of the land' were probably introduced into England by Dutchmen during the late sixteenth century and continued to be an essential part of the farm until tractors replaced the horse. The wagon, like the heavy horse, was a splendid combination of beauty and utility.

Windmills and Watermills

Behold a giant am I
Aloft here in my tower,
With my gentle jaws I devour
The wheat, the maize and the rye.
                                        Longfellow

The most beautiful of the kind I have ever beheld. . . . They are all painted or
washed white, the sails are black; it was a fine morning, the wind was brisk and
their twirling altogether added greatly to the beauty of the scene.
                    William Cobbett, on seeing windmills in Suffolk

Markham's Mill, Snape, a post-mill built on a stout post supported by substructures of cross-beams and transverse stays. The buck (body of the mill) revolved on top of the post so that the sails faced the wind. The framework was sometimes encased in a round house built of brick.

Another view of Markham's Mill. Originally the buck of a post-mill was moved by a tail-beam to bring the sails to face the wind.

Hudson's Mill, Snape, a post-mill which had a round house added. The top was demolished before the Second World War and the round house converted into a dwelling house or a studio by Benjamin Britten. Post-mills predominated in Suffolk, and quite a few round houses still stand although the rest of the mill has gone. An automatic fan-tail to turn the buck of a post-mill was developed during the eighteenth century (this is shown clearly on the right). The fan-tail caught the wind and turned the buck in the right direction for the sails to face the wind. Four sails, as here, were usually preferred. By 1772 the 'spring-sail' was introduced – a system of louvres (rather like venetian blinds) which could be opened or closed by a lever on the sails. This gave the miller some control over the power exercised by the wind. Later the adjustment was done automatically by a rod which went to the grindstones. A bell would warn the miller when there was no more corn in the hopper, because a strong wind and no corn being ground would play havoc with the mill.

Post-mill with roundhouse at Grundisburgh. The mill has been demolished and the round-house converted into a dwelling.

Post-mill with round house at Waldringfield. All remains of this mill have disappeared.

Post-mill seen from Eyke Street. A postman is on his delivery round, a woman is out with a perambulator, a horse and wagon are behind her, and a high-wheeled trap has stopped in the background.

Post-mill at Eyke, 1909. The sails are in disrepair and a greenhouse has been built in front of the mill.

Tricker's Mill, Woodbridge, a tower mill. Only the tower remains. Buttrum's Mill at Woodbridge has been preserved. The machinery is housed in the base (built of brick or stone) and a fan that turns the cap into the wind.

Alderton Mill, which ceased working in 1932, a smock mill. Like the tower mill, only the cap revolves, but the base is of timber and usually octagonally shaped. Its name derives from the resemblance to a miller's flared smock.

The watermill at Wickham Market. This, as with most Suffolk watermills, has an under-shot wheel, with the water striking the blades beneath the wheel and causing it to revolve. With the overshot wheel the water flowed from above and filled the nearest troughs on the wheel, the weight then causing the wheel to revolve. A variation of this called the breast shot wheel made more economical use of the water flow. A windmill once stood close to this watermill. This was quite usual: if there was no wind the miller could use water to do his grinding and vice versa. The miller (his windmill gone) took advantage of another source of power in 1893 by installing a steam-powered roller mill made by Whitmore and Binyon of Wickham.

Watermill at Campsey Ash. This mill was still working in the 1960s. A horse and cart stands by the lucarne which projects from the upper part of the mill and houses the external hoist for lifting the sacks of corn for the bin inside. Latterly these mills only ground wheat, barley and oats, but formerly they also ground rye which, until the beginning of the eighteenth century, provided almost half the flour for breadmaking.

The tide mill, Woodbridge, 1950s. As the tide rose water was collected in a reservoir and stored. The mill could only be worked after the tide had fallen and the miller worked in shifts dictated by the tide. This mill stopped working in 1957.

The ketch barge *Sussex Belle* at the Tide Mill Wharf, Woodbridge in the 1920s. Built of Sussex oak by G. & T. Smith at Rye in 1892, the *Sussex Belle* was a frequent trader to the Deben when owned by Mr Edward Garnham, of Byculia Villa, Belle Vue Road, Ipswich. A very fine example of a 'boomie' barge, she was always considered to be one of the best such coasters and endeared herself to her crew by being a very dry ship. 'The *Sussex Belle* – you could live on her as long as you like,' a Woodbridge seaman once said. In 1910 she was insured with the Harwich Barge Alliance Insurance Association for £1,050, though by 1927 her value had dropped to £900. She was lost in that year while bound from Keadby, on the River Trent, for Orford with a cargo of coal. Taking shelter in Yarmouth Roads from an easterly gale, she dragged her anchor and drove ashore, breaking up under the impact of the waves.

This drainage windmill at Chillesford, 1955, was destroyed by wind on 13 January 1959.
A tower mill with fan-tail, it was used for draining the marshes.

Acknowledgements

A. Berg • K. Burges • Miss Churchyard • Mrs Cooke • S. Cuncliffe • J. Duce
G. Dyke • N. Edgar • Mrs Foster • R.C. Graham • Miss Hatcher
G.W. Holland • Hollesley Bay Colony •D. Kindred • B. Ling • Mrs Locke
P. Maylott • Mrs Morgan • M. Morris • H.P. Pettistree WI • M. Pinney
Mrs Raynor • Red Poll Cattle Society • P. Ryder-Davies • D.C. Shotton
Suffolk Horse Society • J. Tooke • the Waller Collection • M. Watson
B. Wright